Sticky
Steam
Puddings

KÖNEMANN

Perfect Puddings

Agood old-fashioned sticky or steamed pudding is everyone's favourite treat—and they are surprisingly easy to make once you've mastered the basic techniques explained below.

Puddings are the ultimate comfort food, a flashback to childhoods of Sunday roasts, visits to Grandma's—and of course not having to worry about diets. But everyone deserves a treat now and then, and a sticky or steamed pudding is a wonderful indulgence.

As with most things old-fashioned, some of the pudding recipes may take a little extra time to prepare and cook, but the results are worth it. Techniques such as preparing a pudding basin for a traditional steamed pudding may seem complicated, but the photographs on this page will guide you through each step clearly and effortlessly.

The recipes in this book are cooked in a variety of containers, from cake tins to ovenproof dishes to pudding basins. The cake tins are self explanatory, but ovenproof dishes can be glass, ceramic or

metal, as long as you use a container with the cup capacity indicated in the recipe. To test this, stand the dish on a flat surface and pour in water from a measuring cup. Fill it right to the brim—and don't forget to count how many cups it takes.

Pudding basins come in three varieties, ceramic, aluminium or glass. They are available from kitchen shops, department stores and some hardware stores.

Aluminium and ceramic pudding basins.

Aluminium pudding basins come with a lid which clips on securely, while ceramic and glass pudding basins don't, and must be covered as directed, to make sure that they are watertight.

It is a good idea to brush the inside of the basin with oil or melted butter as you would a cake tin, so that the pudding doesn't stick when you try to turn it out. Some recipes will say to line the base with baking paper.

Line the base with baking paper.

Obviously the base of a pudding basin is quite small, but that little circle of baking paper can mean the difference between an impressive 'turn out', and a mess.

The next step is to prepare the top covering. Brush a sheet of foil with melted butter or oil and lay a sheet of baking paper (which is non-stick) on the oiled side of the foil. The oil holds the sheets together. Make a wide pleat in the centre, this allows the covering to expand as the pudding cooks and rises.

Lay the pleated foil and paper over the basin.

When the pudding mixture has been spooned into the prepared basin, cover the top with the baking paper and foil, foil-side-up. If you are using an aluminium pudding basin, simply clip the lid on now. If you are using a ceramic or glass basin, place a clean pleated tea towel over the foil and tie

Tie the tea towel on securely.

kitchen string under the basin lip; knot securely.

Bring the four corners of the tea towel up and tie them

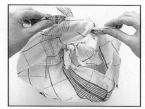

Tie the corners of the tea towel together.

together—you can use this as a handle to help you lower the basin into the cooking pot.

Next, place a trivet (a small heatproof stand), or an upturned saucer in the base of a large pan. Sit the basin on the trivet, and carefully pour in enough boiling water to come about halfway up the side of

Pour boiling water into the pan.

the pudding basin. Take care not to splash the top of the pudding. Place the pan over the heat, cover and cook as directed. Don't forget to check the pan from time to time, as the water may get low or even boil dry. Make sure that

you always top up the pan with BOILING water, so that the cooking time remains constant.

Test the pudding with a skewer.

After the given cooking time, remove the basin from the pan of water, and remove the coverings. Insert a skewer into the centre of the pudding—if it comes out clean the pudding is cooked. Remember that steamed puddings are supposed to be moist, so don't be tempted to overcook. If the pudding does need more time, cover it again (use the same foil/paper—don't worry if the covering is a little rough at this stage) and cook for a little longer. When the pudding is done, remove the coverings completely and leave it to stand for about 5 minutes. Turn the pudding out onto a serving plate and cut into wedges to serve.

Sticky and Steamed Puddings

Arich and sticky warming pudding or something light and fruity? The only problem is which to try first.

Caramel, Macadamia and Coconut Pudding

Preparation Time:
  35 minutes
Total Cooking Time:
  1 hour
Serves 6–8

3/4 cup (140 g/4²/3 oz)
  lightly packed soft
  brown sugar
1/4 cup (60 ml/2 fl oz)
  cream
60 g (2 oz) butter, melted
1 cup (135 g/4¹/2 oz)
  chopped macadamia
  nuts
1/2 cup (30 g/1 oz)
  shredded coconut
90 g (3 oz) butter
1/2 cup (125 g/4 oz)
  caster sugar
2 eggs, lightly beaten
1 teaspoon vanilla
  essence
1 cup (125 g/4 oz) self-
  raising flour
1/3 cup (80 ml/2³/4 fl oz)
  milk

1. Preheat the oven to 180°C (350°F/Gas 4). Lightly brush a 20 cm (8 inch) round, deep ovenproof dish with melted butter or oil; line the base with baking paper. Combine the brown sugar, cream and melted butter; pour into the dish. Place the nuts and coconut on a baking tray and toast in the oven for 3–5 minutes until golden brown; stirring frequently. Sprinkle over the mixture in the dish.
2. Beat the butter and sugar until light and creamy. Gradually add the eggs and vanilla, beating well after each addition. Fold in the sifted flour alternately with the milk. Spoon into the dish.
3. Bake for 45–50 minutes, or until a skewer inserted into the middle of the pudding comes out clean. Turn out and serve.

Caramel, Macadamia and Coconut Pudding

Sticky Chocolate Espresso Pudding

Preparation time:
  30 minutes
Total cooking time:
  1 hour
Serves 8–10

125 g (4 oz) butter
1 cup (185 g/6 oz)
  lightly packed
  soft brown sugar
1/2 cup (125 g/4 oz)
  caster sugar
3 eggs
1 1/2 tablespoons
  instant coffee powder
2 cups (250 g/8 oz)
  plain flour
1/2 cup (60 g/2 oz)
  cocoa powder
1 teaspoon bicarbonate
  of soda
1/2 cup (125 g/4 oz)
  sour cream

Coffee Cream Sauce
1/4 cup (60 g/2 oz)
  caster sugar
1/2 cup (95 g/3 1/4 oz)
  lightly packed soft
  brown sugar
1 cup (250 ml/8 fl oz)
  cream
1 1/2 tablespoons
  instant coffee powder
2 tablespoons Tia
  Maria, optional
thick cream, to serve

1. Preheat the oven to 180°C (350°F/Gas 4). Lightly brush a 25 cm (10 inch) round springform tin with melted butter or oil; line the base with baking paper.
2. Using electric beaters, beat the butter and sugars together until light and creamy. Add the eggs one at a time, beating well after each addition. Dissolve the instant coffee powder in 2/3 cup (170 ml/5 1/2 fl oz) hot water. Using a metal spoon, gently fold the coffee liquid into the butter mixture alternately with the sifted flour, cocoa and bicarbonate of soda. Fold in the sour cream. Mix until all the ingredients are just combined; be careful not to overbeat.
3. Carefully spoon the mixture into the prepared tin and smooth the surface. Bake for 55 minutes, or until a skewer comes out clean when inserted into the centre of the pudding. Cover the pudding with foil for the last 15 minutes of baking if it starts becoming too brown on top. While the pudding is cooking make the sauce.
4. To make Coffee Cream Sauce: Combine the caster sugar, brown sugar, cream and instant coffee powder in a small pan. Stir over medium heat, without boiling, until the sugars have completely dissolved. Bring to the boil, reduce the heat, and simmer, uncovered, for about 3 minutes, or until the mixture has thickened slightly. Stir in the Tia Maria, if you are using it.
5. Remove the pudding from the oven and while it is still hot, brush the top with a little of the Coffee Cream Sauce. Allow the pudding to cool slightly before removing it from the tin. Place the pudding on a serving plate and brush it again with the sauce. Serve warm, cut into wedges and drizzled with the remaining Coffee Cream Sauce and some thick cream, if you like.

HINT
When testing puddings with a skewer, avoid inserting the skewer into any cracks as this will usually show a very moist crumb. Always insert the skewer into a smooth surface.

Sticky Chocolate Espresso Pudding

Fig and Ginger Pudding

Preparation time:
30 minutes +
30 minutes standing
Total cooking time:
50 minutes
Serves 8

1¹/4 cups (230 g/
7¹/3 oz) finely
chopped dried figs
¹/2 cup (125 ml/4 fl oz)
green ginger wine
1 teaspoon bicarbonate
of soda
60 g (2 oz) butter
³/4 cup (185 g/6 oz)
caster sugar
2 eggs
1 cup (125 g/4 oz)
self-raising flour
2 teaspoons ground
ginger
¹/4 cup (30 g/1 oz)
chopped walnuts
¹/2 cup (50 g/1²/3 oz)
walnut halves, for
decoration

1. Preheat the oven to 180°C (350°F/Gas 4). Lightly brush a 20 cm (8 inch) round cake tin with melted butter or oil; line the base with baking paper.
2. Combine the figs, wine and ¹/2 cup (125 ml/4 fl oz) water in a bowl; cover and leave for 30 minutes. Pour the fig mixture into a small pan and bring to the boil, add the bicarbonate of soda and stir to combine (the mixture will become frothy). Remove from heat and set aside for 5 minutes.
3. Beat the butter and sugar with electric beaters until light and creamy. Add the eggs one at a time, beating well between each addition. Using a large metal spoon, fold in the sifted flour and ginger alternately with the fig mixture; fold in the chopped walnuts.
4. Pour the mixture into the prepared tin. Decorate the outside edge of the pudding with walnut halves, keeping to the edge so that the pudding doesn't dip in the middle. Bake for 50 minutes, or until a skewer inserted into the centre of the pudding comes out clean. Leave the pudding in the tin for 5 minutes before turning out onto a wire rack to cool. Transfer to a serving plate and dust with icing sugar. Serve warm with cream.

Note: Avoid opening the oven during cooking: this pudding is quite delicate and may dip a little in the centre.

Fig and Ginger Pudding

1 *Line the base of a 20 cm (8 inch) round tin with baking paper.*

2 *Stir in the bicarbonate of soda; the mixture will become frothy.*

3 Add the eggs one at a time, beating well between each addition.

4 Decorate the outer edge of the pudding with walnut halves.

Sticky Passionfruit and Berry Pudding

Preparation time:
  30 minutes
Total cooking time:
  1 hour
Serves 8

1/4 cup (45 g/1^1/2 oz)
  ground almonds
2 tablespoons caster
  sugar
400 g (12^2/3 oz) fresh
  blackberries,
  boysenberries or
  raspberries
  (see Note)
185 g (6 oz) butter
2/3 cup (160 g/5^1/4 oz)
  caster sugar, extra
3 eggs
3/4 cup (90 g/3 oz) self-
  raising flour
3/4 cup (90 g/3 oz)
  plain flour
1/2 cup (95 g/3^1/4 oz)
  ground almonds,
  extra
1/2 cup (125 ml/4 fl oz)
  milk

Passionfruit Sauce
3/4 cup (185 g/6 oz)
  fresh passionfruit pulp
  (see Note)
1/2 cup (125 g/4 fl oz)
  water
1/3 cup (90 g/3 oz)
  sugar
3/4 cup (185 ml/6 fl oz)
  cream

*Sticky Passionfruit and Berry Pudding with
Passionfruit Sauce*

1. Preheat the oven to
180°C (350°F/Gas 4).
Lightly brush a 23 cm
(9 inch) round cake tin
with melted butter or
oil and line the base
with baking paper.
Combine the ground
almonds with the sugar
and sprinkle the
mixture evenly over the
base of the prepared
tin. Sprinkle the berries
over the almond
mixture.
2. Beat the butter and
the extra sugar together
using electric beaters
until the mixture is
light and creamy. Add
the eggs one at a time,
beating well after each
addition. Fold in the
sifted flours and the
extra ground almonds
alternately with the
milk.
3. Carefully spoon the
butter mixture over the
almond mixture and
the berries in the
prepared tin and
smooth the top. Bake
for about 50 minutes,
or until a skewer
inserted into the centre
of the pudding comes
out clean. Leave the
pudding in the tin for
at least 5 minutes
before turning it out
onto a wire rack.
Transfer to a serving
plate.

**4. To make the
Passionfruit Sauce:**
Combine the
passionfruit pulp, water
and sugar in a pan and
stir over medium heat
without boiling until
the sugar has
completely dissolved.
Bring to the boil.
Reduce the heat and
simmer, uncovered and
without stirring, for
2 to 3 minutes or until
it has thickened slightly.
Reserve 1/4 cup of the
passionfuit syrup
mixture to brush over
the pudding. Add the
cream to the syrup
remaining in the pan
and bring to the boil.
Remove the pan from
the heat and pour the
sauce into a heatproof
jug for serving.
5. Brush the reserved
passionfruit syrup over
the pudding while it is
still hot. Serve the
pudding warm or at
room temperature with
the warm Passionfruit
Sauce.

Note: Only fresh
berries should be
used for this pudding.
You can use any one
of the varieties
suggested or any
combination. You will
need about 10 large
fresh passionfruit to
provide enough
passionfruit pulp to
make the sauce.

Banana Pudding with Passionfruit Cream

Preparation time:
  20 minutes
Total cooking time:
  2 hours 30 minutes
Serves 6

 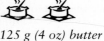

125 g (4 oz) butter
1/2 cup (125 g/4 oz)
  caster sugar
1 teaspoon vanilla
  essence
2 eggs
3/4 cup (90 g/3 oz) self-
  raising flour
1/4 cup (60 g/2 oz) plain
  flour
1/2 teaspoon
  bicarbonate of soda
1 cup (240 g/7 1/2 oz)
  mashed banana

Passionfruit Cream
250 g (8 oz) mascarpone
1/4 cup (60 g/2 oz) fresh
  passionfruit pulp
  (see Note)
2 tablespoons icing sugar

1. Brush a 6 cup
(1.5 litre) capacity
pudding basin with
melted butter or oil; line
the base with baking
paper. Brush a large
sheet of foil with melted
butter or oil. Lay a
sheet of baking paper
over the greased side of
the foil. Pleat along the
centre.
2. Beat the butter, sugar
and vanilla until light
and creamy. Add the
eggs one at a time; beat
well after each addition.
Fold in the sifted dry
ingredients alternately
with the banana. Pour
into the basin. Cover
with the foil and paper,
foil-side-up. Place the
lid over the foil; secure
clips. If you don't have
a lid, lay a pleated tea
towel over the foil, tie
with string and knot the
corners together to act
as a handle.
3. Place the basin on a
trivet or upturned
saucer in a deep pan.
Pour in boiling water to
come halfway up the
basin. Bring to the boil,
reduce the heat and
simmer, covered, for
2 hours 30 minutes, or
until a skewer comes
out clean. Add boiling
water as needed. Leave
for 5 minutes before
turning out. Dust with
icing sugar. Serve warm
with Passionfruit Cream.
5. To make Passionfruit
Cream: Stir the
mascarpone in a bowl
to soften it; stir in the
passionfruit pulp and
icing sugar until just
combined—if overmixed
it will curdle. Serve
immediately.

Note: You will need
about 3 large bananas
and 4 passionfruit for
this recipe.

Butterscotch Pudding

Preparation time:
  30 minutes
Cooking time:
  1 hour–1 hour 15
  minutes
Serves 6–8

125 g (4 oz) butter,
  softened
1/2 cup (115 g/3 3/4 oz)
  firmly packed soft
  brown sugar
2 eggs
1/4 cup (90 g/3 oz)
  golden syrup
2 cups (250 g/8 oz) self-
  raising flour
3/4 cup (185 ml/6 fl oz)
  cream
strawberries, to serve

Butterscotch Sauce
100 g (3 1/3 oz) butter
1/2 cup (115 g/3 3/4 oz)
  firmly packed soft
  brown sugar
1/2 cup (125 ml/4 fl oz)
  cream

1. Preheat the oven to
180°C (350°F/Gas 4).
Lightly brush a deep
20 cm (8 inch) round
tin with melted butter
or oil; line the base
with baking paper.
Brush a large sheet of
foil with melted butter
or oil. Lay a sheet of
baking paper over the
greased side of the foil,
pleat along the centre.

Banana Pudding with Passionfruit Cream (top) and Butterscotch Pudding

2. Beat the butter and sugar until light and creamy. Add the eggs one at a time, beating well between additions. Add the golden syrup; mix well. The mixture may appear curdled at this stage.

3. Fold in the sifted flour alternately with the cream. Spoon the mixture into the tin. Cover with greased foil and paper, foil-side-up. Secure with string and place in a large baking dish. Pour in water to come halfway up the pudding tin and bake for 1 hour–1¹/4 hours, until a skewer inserted into the centre of the pudding comes out clean. Turn out and serve with Butterscotch Sauce. Decorate with strawberries.

4. **To make Butterscotch Sauce:** Place the butter and sugar in a pan. Stir over a low heat until the butter has melted and the sugar dissolved. Gradually stir in the cream.

Honey Lemon Pudding with Citrus Marmalade

Preparation time:
  1 hour + cooling time
Total cooking time:
  2 hours 40 minutes
Serves 6

180 g (5³/4 oz) butter
¹/4 cup (60 g/2 oz)
  caster sugar
³/4 cup (260 g/8¹/3 oz)
  honey
¹/4 cup (60 ml/2 fl oz)
  lemon juice
2 eggs
1¹/2 cups (185 g/6 oz)
  plain flour
1¹/2 cups (185 g/6 oz)
  self-raising flour
1 teaspoon bicarbonate
  of soda
2 tablespoons grated
  lemon rind

Citrus Marmalade
4 oranges
2 limes
2 small grapefruit
¹/2 cup (125 g/4 oz)
  sugar
2 tablespoons honey

1. Lightly brush a 6 cup (1.5 litre) capacity pudding basin with butter or melted oil; line the base with baking paper. Brush a large sheet of foil with melted butter or oil. Lay a sheet of baking paper over the greased side of the foil. Pleat them along the centre.

2. Combine the butter, sugar, honey and lemon juice in a pan and stir over medium heat until the butter has melted. Pour the mixture into a heatproof bowl and cool to room temperature.

3. Using a wire whisk, beat the eggs into the cooled mixture, add the sifted flours and bicarbonate of soda and the lemon rind. Stir until smooth. Pour the mixture into the prepared pudding basin, cover with the greased foil and paper, foil-side-up. Place the lid over the foil and secure the clips. If you don't have a lid, place a pleated tea towel over the foil, tie securely with string under the lip of the basin and knot the four corners together; this acts as a handle to help lower the basin into the pan. Place the basin on a trivet or an upturned saucer in a large, deep pan.

4. Carefully pour boiling water down the side of the pan to come halfway up the side of the basin. Bring to the boil, reduce the heat slightly and simmer, covered, for about 2 hours, or until a skewer inserted into the centre of the pudding comes out clean. Add more boiling water to the pan as necessary: do not let it boil dry. Leave the pudding in the basin for 5 minutes before turning it out onto a serving plate. Serve the pudding warm or at room temperature with Citrus Marmalade and cream, if desired.

5. To make the Citrus Marmalade: Remove the rind and all the pith from the oranges, limes and grapefruit. Divide them into segments: using a sharp knife cut carefully between the membrane and the flesh. Combine the fruit segments and the sugar in a large pan and cook over low heat for a few minutes or until the sugar has completely dissolved. Increase the heat slightly and allow the mixture to simmer uncovered for about 35 minutes or until it becomes thick and syrupy; stir in the honey. Transfer the marmalade to a heatproof bowl and allow to cool.

Honey Lemon Pudding with Citrus Marmalade

Lime and Coconut Pudding with Summer Fruit Salad

Preparation time:
  30 minutes
Total cooking time:
  2 hours
Serves 6

125 g (4 oz) butter
3/4 cup (185 g/6 oz)
  caster sugar
1 tablespoon finely
  grated lime rind
2 eggs
1/2 cup (45 g/1 1/2 oz)
  desiccated coconut
1 1/2 cups (185 g/6 oz)
  self-raising flour
1/2 cup (125 ml/4 fl oz)
  lime juice

Summer Fruit Salad
2 1/2 tablespoons lime
  juice
1 1/4 cups (310 g/9 3/4 oz)
  coconut cream
1 1/2 tablespoons
  honey
2 peaches, sliced into
  thin wedges
2 kiwi fruit, sliced
  lengthways into
  wedges
400 g (12 2/3 oz) red
  papaya, sliced
2 bananas, sliced
  diagonally

1. Lightly brush a 6 cup (1.5 litre) capacity pudding basin with melted butter or oil; dust with flour and line the base with baking paper. Brush a large sheet of foil with melted butter or oil. Lay a sheet of baking paper over the greased side of the foil. Pleat them along the centre.
2. Using electric beaters, beat the butter and sugar in a bowl until light and creamy. Add the lime rind and beat until thoroughly combined. Add the eggs one at a time, beating well between additions. Using a large metal spoon, fold in the coconut and the sifted flour alternately with the lime juice.
3. Spoon the mixture into the prepared pudding basin. Smooth the surface and cover with the greased foil and paper, foil-side-up. Place the lid over the foil and secure the clips. If you don't have a lid, lay a pleated tea towel over the foil, tie securely with string under the lip of the basin and knot the four corners together; this acts as a handle to help you lower the basin into the pan. Place the basin on a trivet or an upturned saucer in a large, deep pan. Carefully pour boiling water down the side of the pan to come halfway up the side of the basin. Bring to the boil, reduce the heat slightly and simmer, covered, for 2 hours, or until a skewer inserted into the centre of the pudding comes out clean. Leave the pudding in the basin for 5 minutes before turning out onto a serving plate.
4. To make Summer Fruit Salad: Place the lime juice, coconut cream and honey in a jug and whisk together with a fork or small wire whisk. Prepare the fruit just before serving, and spoon it onto the serving plates next to a wedge of the pudding. Pour the coconut cream mixture over the fruit and around the pudding.

HINT
If using a tea towel to cover the pudding basin, wear rubber gloves when lifting it from the pan. This makes it easier to grip the basin and helps prevent steam burns.

Lime and Coconut Pudding with
Summer Fruit Salad

1 Line the bases of the heatproof moulds with baking paper.

2 Fold the chocolate chips and apple into the pudding mixture.

Chocolate Puddings with Muscat Cream

Preparation time:
20 minutes
Total cooking time:
40 minutes
Serves 6

1/2 teaspoon
bicarbonate of soda
1/2 cup (125 ml/4 fl oz)
milk
125 g (4 oz) butter
2/3 cup (155 g/5 oz)
firmly packed soft
brown sugar
2 eggs, lightly beaten
1 1/4 cups (155 g/5 oz)
self-raising flour
1/3 cup (40 g/1 1/3 oz)
cocoa powder
125 g (4 oz) dark
chocolate chips
1 Granny Smith
apple, peeled and
coarsely grated

Muscat Cream
2 eggs, separated
1/4 cup (60 g/2 oz)
caster sugar
1/4 cup (60 ml/2 fl oz)
liqueur Muscat or
Tokay
1 cup (250 ml/8 fl oz)
cream, whipped

1. Preheat the oven to 180°C (350°F/Gas 4). Brush six 1 cup (250 ml/8 fl oz) capacity heatproof moulds with melted butter or oil; line the bases with baking paper. Brush 6 small sheets of foil with melted butter or oil. Lay a sheet of baking paper over the greased side of each piece of foil; pleat down the centre. Dissolve the soda in the milk.
2. Beat the butter and sugar with electric beaters until light and creamy. Add the eggs gradually, beating well after each addition. Fold in the sifted flour and cocoa alternately with the milk mixture. Fold in the chocolate chips and apple.
3. Spoon the mixture into the moulds. Cover with foil and paper, foil-side-up, and tie with string. Place in a large baking dish. Pour in enough boiling water to come halfway up the moulds. Bake for 40 minutes, or until a skewer inserted into the centre of a pudding comes out clean. Turn out and decorate with chocolate shavings, if desired. Serve with Muscat Cream.
4. **To make Muscat Cream:** Beat the egg yolks and sugar until thick and creamy. Beat the egg whites until soft peaks form. Stir in the Muscat, then fold in the egg whites and cream.

Chocolate Puddings with Muscat Cream

3 Pour boiling water down the side of the dish to come halfway up the moulds.

4 Beat the egg yolks and sugar until thick and creamy.

19

Polenta Puddings with Apricot Sauce

Preparation time:
 25 minutes
Total cooking time:
 1 hour
Serves 6

125 g (4 oz) butter
$2/3$ cup (160 g/$5^1/4$ oz)
 caster sugar
2 eggs, lightly
 beaten
2 teaspoons finely
 chopped lemon
 rind
1 cup (125 g/4 oz)
 self-raising flour
$1/2$ teaspoon baking
 powder
$1/4$ teaspoon salt
$2/3$ cup (100 g/
 $3^1/2$ oz) polenta
 (see Note)
$1/2$ cup (125 g/4 fl oz)
 thick sour cream
$1/3$ cup (80 ml/
 $2^3/4$ fl oz) milk

Apricot Sauce
125 g (4 oz) dried
 apricots, roughly
 chopped
1 cup (250 ml/8 fl oz)
 apple juice
3 wide strips lemon
 rind, white pith
 removed
$1/4$ cup (60 g/2 oz)
 sugar
1 tablespoon Cointreau
 (optional)

1. Preheat the oven to 180°C (350°F/Gas 4). Lightly brush six 1 cup (250 ml/8 fl oz) capacity heatproof moulds with melted butter or oil; line the bases with baking paper. Brush 6 small sheets of foil with melted butter or oil. Lay a small sheet of baking paper over the greased side of each piece of foil and make a pleat down the centre.
2. Beat the butter and sugar with electric beaters until light and creamy. Add the eggs gradually, beating thoroughly after each addition. Beat in the lemon rind. Using a large metal spoon, fold in the sifted flour and baking powder, salt and polenta alternately with the combined sour cream and milk.
3. Spoon the mixture evenly into the moulds, filling them three-quarters full. Cover each mould with a piece of greased foil and paper, foil-side-up. Tie with string. Place the moulds in a large deep baking dish. Carefully pour boiling water down the side of the dish to come half-way up the sides of the moulds. Bake for about 40–50 minutes, or until a skewer inserted into the centre of a pudding comes out clean. Turn the puddings out of their moulds and serve with warm Apricot Sauce.
4. To make Apricot Sauce: Place the apricots in a pan with the apple juice, 1 cup (250 ml/8 fl oz) of water and the strips of lemon rind; bring to the boil. Reduce the heat, partially cover the pan and simmer for about 10 minutes, or until the apricots are tender. Remove the lemon rind, then add the sugar and stir until it is completely dissolved. Allow the sauce to cool for 10 minutes then transfer it to a food processor and process until smooth. Stir in the Cointreau.

Note: Polenta is available from supermarkets or health food stores and is sometimes known as cornmeal (not to be confused with cornflour). Polenta is bright yellow and some brands are coarser than others. Try to choose a cornmeal that is not too coarse.

Polenta Puddings with Apricot Sauce

Sago Plum Pudding with Rum Butter

Preparation time:
30–35 minutes +
overnight soaking
Total cooking time:
3¹/2–4 hours
Serves 6–8

¹/3 cup (65 g/2¹/4 oz)
sago
1 cup (250 ml/8 fl oz)
milk
1 teaspoon bicarbonate
of soda
³/4 cup (140 g/4²/3 oz)
lightly packed dark
brown sugar
2 cups (160 g/5¹/4 oz)
fresh white
breadcrumbs
¹/2 cup (60 g/2 oz)
sultanas
¹/2 cup (75 g/2¹/2 oz)
currants
¹/2 cup (90 g/3 oz)
dates, chopped
2 eggs, lightly
beaten
60 g (2 oz) butter,
melted
raspberries, blueberries
and icing sugar for
decoration

Rum Butter
125 g (4 oz) butter,
softened
³/4 cup (140 g/4²/3 oz)
lightly packed dark
brown sugar
4 tablespoons rum

1. Combine the sago and milk in a small bowl, cover and refrigerate overnight. Lightly brush a 6 cup (1.5 litre) capacity pudding basin with melted butter or oil and line the base with baking paper. Brush a large sheet of foil with melted butter or oil. Lay a sheet of baking paper over the greased side of the foil. Pleat them along the centre.

2. Place the soaked sago and milk in a large mixing bowl and stir through the bicarbonate of soda until dissolved. Stir in the brown sugar, breadcrumbs, dried fruit, beaten eggs and melted butter and mix together well.

3. Spoon the mixture into the basin and smooth the surface. Cover with the greased foil and paper, foil-side-up. Place the lid over the foil and secure the clips. If you don't have a lid, lay a pleated tea towel over the foil and tie it securely with string under the lip of the basin. Knot the four corners together; this acts as a handle and will help you to lower the basin into the pan.

4. Place the basin on a trivet or an upturned saucer in a large, deep pan. Carefully pour boiling water down the side of the pan to come halfway up the side of the basin. Bring the water back to the boil, reduce the heat slightly, cover and simmer for 3¹/2–4 hours, or until a skewer inserted into the centre of the pudding comes out clean. Add more boiling water to the pan as necessary: don't let it boil dry. Remove the basin from the pan, remove the coverings and leave for 5 minutes before turning the pudding out onto a large serving plate. Decorate with raspberries and blueberries, dust with icing sugar and serve hot with cold Rum Butter.

5. **To make Rum Butter:** Beat together the butter and brown sugar with electric beaters for about 3–4 minutes, or until light and creamy. Gradually beat in the rum, one tablespoon at a time. Add more rum to taste, if liked. Place the Rum Butter in a serving dish, cover and refrigerate until required.

Sago Plum Pudding with Rum Butter

22

Fig Pudding with Brandy Sauce

Preparation time:
40 minutes +
2 hours standing
Total cooking time:
4 hours 10 minutes
Serves 8–10

1¹/2 cups (240 g/
7¹/2 oz) soft dessert
figs, chopped
1¹/4 cups (225 g/
7¹/4 oz) pitted dates,
chopped
³/4 cup (90 g/3 oz)
raisins
¹/3 cup (80 g/2²/3 oz)
glacé ginger, chopped
2 tablespoons brandy
or orange juice
¹/4 cup (45 g/1¹/2 oz)
lightly packed soft
brown sugar
3 cups (240 g/7¹/2 oz)
fresh white
breadcrumbs
2 cups (250 g/8 oz) self-
raising flour, sifted
160 g (5¹/4 oz) butter,
melted
3 eggs, lightly beaten
¹/2 cup (125 ml/4 fl oz)
milk
2 teaspoons grated
lemon rind
3 tablespoons lemon
juice

Brandy Sauce
¹/4 cup (30 g/1 oz)
cornflour
¹/4 cup (60 g/2 oz)
caster sugar

2 cups (500 ml/16 fl oz)
milk
30 g (1 oz) butter
¹/3 cup (80 ml/
2³/4 fl oz) brandy

1. Brush an 8 cup
(2 litre) capacity
pudding basin with
melted butter or oil;
line the base with
baking paper. Brush a
large sheet of foil with
melted butter or oil.
Lay a sheet of baking
paper over the greased
side of the foil. Pleat
them along the centre.
Combine the figs,
dates, raisins and
ginger in a bowl. Stir in
the brandy or orange
juice and set aside for
at least 2 hours.
2. Combine the brown
sugar, breadcrumbs and
sifted flour. Stir in the
soaked fruit then add
the butter, eggs, milk,
lemon rind and juice;
stir until evenly mixed.
Spoon into the basin
and press firmly to
eliminate any air
bubbles. Smooth the
surface and cover with
the greased foil and
paper, foil-side-up.
Place the lid over the
foil and secure the
clips. If you don't have
a lid, lay a pleated tea
towel over the foil, tie
with string under the
lip of the basin and

knot the four corners
together; this acts as a
handle to help lower
the basin into the pan.
3. Place the basin on a
trivet in a large, deep
pan. Pour boiling water
down the side of the
pan to come halfway
up the side of the basin.
Bring to the boil, reduce
the heat slightly, cover
and simmer for 4 hours,
or until a skewer
inserted into the centre
of the pudding comes
out clean. Remove the
basin from the water,
remove the coverings
and leave for 5 minutes
before turning out onto
a serving plate. Dust
with icing sugar. Serve
hot, with hot Brandy
Sauce. Decorate with
fresh figs, if desired.
4. **To make Brandy
Sauce:** Combine the
cornflour and sugar in
a pan, add a little milk
and mix to a smooth
paste. Add the
remaining milk and
whisk over medium
heat for 3–4 minutes
until the sauce is
smooth and thick. Stir
in the butter and
brandy. Serve hot.

Note: Soft dessert figs
are dried figs that have
been tenderised. They
are available in
supermarkets.

Fig Pudding with Brandy Sauce

Upside-down Tamarillo Pudding with Passionfruit Cream

Preparation time:
  35 minutes
Total cooking time:
  1 hour–1 hour 10
  minutes
Serves 6–8

3–4 tamarillos
125 g (4 oz) butter
3/4 cup (185 g/6 oz)
  caster sugar
2 eggs, *lightly beaten*
1 teaspoon vanilla
  essence
13/4 cups (220 g/7 oz)
  self-raising flour
1/4 cup (45 g/11/2 oz)
  almond meal
1/2 cup (125 g/4 oz)
  sour cream
2 tablespoons milk

Passionfruit Cream
1/3 cup (90 g/3 oz)
  passionfruit pulp
1 cup (250 ml/8 fl oz)
  cream, *whipped*

1. Preheat the oven to 180°C (350°F/Gas 4). Lightly brush a deep 20 cm (8 inch) round ovenproof dish with melted butter or oil; line the base with baking paper. Cut a cross in the base of each tamarillo, place them in a bowl and cover with boiling water, leave for 5 minutes. Remove the tamarillos with a slotted spoon and carefully peel away the skin. Cut them into slices about 5 mm (1/4 inch) thick.

2. Arrange the tamarillo slices over the bottom of the prepared dish. Beat the butter and sugar in a small bowl with electric beaters until light and creamy. Gradually add the eggs and vanilla essence, beating well after each addition. Transfer the mixture to a large mixing bowl.

3. Fold in the sifted flour and almond meal alternately with the combined sour cream and milk, until they are just combined. Carefully spoon the pudding mixture over the top of the tamarillos in the baking dish. Bake for 1 hour to 1 hour 10 minutes, or until a skewer inserted into the centre of the pudding comes out clean. Leave in the baking dish for 5 minutes before turning the pudding out onto a serving plate. Serve with Passionfruit Cream.

4. To make Passionfruit Cream: Gently fold the passionfruit pulp through the whipped cream.

Tipsy Sticky Date Pudding

Preparation time:
  20 minutes
Total cooking time:
  50 minutes
Serves 6

3/4 cup (135 g/41/2 oz)
  dates, *pitted and
  roughly chopped*
1 teaspoon bicarbonate
  of soda
50 g (12/3 oz) soft butter
2/3 cup (155 g/5 oz)
  firmly packed soft
  brown sugar
2 eggs
11/2 cups (185 g/6 oz)
  plain flour
1/2 teaspoon baking
  powder
1 cup (100 g/32/3 oz)
  walnut halves,
  roughly chopped

Syrup
2/3 cup (155 g/5 oz)
  firmly packed soft
  brown sugar
10 g (1/3 oz) butter
1 teaspoon vanilla
  essence
1/3 cup (80 ml/23/4 fl oz)
  brandy

1. Preheat the oven to 180°C (350°F/Gas 4). Lightly brush a deep 6 cup (1.5 litre) capacity ovenproof dish with melted butter or oil. Place the dates and soda in a bowl and pour

*Upside-down Tamarillo Pudding with Passionfruit Cream (top)
and Tipsy Sticky Date Pudding*

over 1 cup (250 ml/
8 fl oz) boiling water.
Set aside to cool (the
mixture will become
foamy). Beat the butter
and sugar with electric
beaters until light and
creamy. Add the eggs
one at a time, beating
well between each
addition.
2. Fold in the sifted

flour and baking
powder, walnuts and
date mixture. Stir until
all the ingredients are
just combined and pour
into the prepared dish.
Bake for 40 minutes, or
until slightly risen and
firm to touch.
3. While the pudding is
cooking prepare the
syrup: place the sugar,

butter, vanilla, brandy
and $1/3$ cup (80 ml/
$2^3/4$ fl oz) water in a
pan and simmer for
5 minutes. Prick a few
holes in the pudding
with a skewer; pour the
syrup over. Return to
the oven for 5 minutes
while the sauce soaks
in. Serve with cream or
natural yoghurt.

27

Golden Syrup Pudding with Sour Cream Vanilla Custard

Preparation time:
  30 minutes
Total cooking time:
  1 hour 20 minutes
Serves 6–8

4 tablespoons golden
  syrup
185 g (6 oz) butter,
  softened
3/4 cup (185 g/6 oz)
  caster sugar
1 teaspoon vanilla
  essence
3 eggs
1/2 cup (60 g/2 oz)
  plain flour
1 cup (125 g/4 oz)
  self-raising flour
1/4 cup (90 g/3 oz)
  warmed golden syrup,
  extra, to serve
strawberries, to serve

**Sour Cream Vanilla
  Custard**
2 tablespoons custard
  powder
2 tablespoons caster
  sugar
1 1/4 cups (315 ml/
  10 fl oz) milk
1 cup (250 g/8 oz)
  sour cream
2 teaspoons vanilla
  essence

1. Preheat the oven to 180°C (350°F/Gas 4). Lightly brush a 20 cm (8 inch) deep round tin with melted butter or oil; line the base and sides with baking paper. Brush a large sheet of foil with melted butter or oil. Lay a sheet of baking paper over the greased side of the foil. Pleat them along the centre.
2. Pour the golden syrup into the bottom of the prepared tin. Beat the butter and sugar with electric beaters until creamy. Add the vanilla essence, eggs and the combined sifted flours to the butter. Beat on a low speed until they are thoroughly mixed, increase the speed to medium and beat for 2 more minutes.
3. Spoon the mixture into the prepared tin and smooth the surface. Cover with the greased foil and paper, foil-side-up, and secure with string.
4. Place the tin in a large deep baking dish. Carefully pour boiling water down the side of the dish to come halfway up the sides of the tin. Bake for 1 hour– 1 hour 15 minutes, or until a skewer inserted into the centre of the pudding comes out clean. Remove the tin from the water, remove the coverings, and leave the pudding to stand for 5 minutes before turning it out onto a large serving plate. Pour the extra warmed golden syrup over the top of the pudding and decorate with strawberries. Serve cut into slices with hot Sour Cream Vanilla Custard.
5. **To make Sour Cream Vanilla Custard:** Combine the custard powder and sugar in a pan and add a little milk to form a smooth paste. Add the remaining milk, sour cream and vanilla essence. Whisk over low heat for about 3–4 minutes or until the custard is thickened and smooth. Allow to simmer for 1 minute more. Cover the custard and reheat gently to serve.

HINT
Place a disc of baking paper on the surface of the custard to prevent a skin forming while it is standing.

Golden Syrup Pudding with Sour Cream Vanilla Custard

Chocolate Eve's Pudding with Chocolate Custard

Preparation time:
  40 minutes
Total cooking time:
  1 hour 20 minutes
Serves 6–8

2 green apples, peeled,
  cored and sliced
1 tablespoon caster
  sugar

Pudding Batter
100 g (3¹/3 oz) dark
  chocolate bits
100 g (3¹/3 oz) butter,
  softened
4 eggs, separated
¹/3 cup (90 g/3 oz)
  caster sugar
1 tablespoon milk
¹/2 cup (60 g/2 oz) plain
  flour, sifted
2 teaspoons cocoa
  powder
¹/4 teaspoon
  bicarbonate of soda
1 cup (80 g/2²/3 oz)
  fresh white breadcrumbs

Chocolate Custard
2 tablespoons custard
  powder
1 tablespoon caster
  sugar
1 teaspoon cocoa
  powder
2 cups (500 ml/16 fl oz)
  milk
100 g (3¹/3 oz) dark
  chocolate bits

1. Lightly brush a
23 cm (9 inch) fluted
ring tin with melted
butter or oil. Brush a
large sheet of foil with
melted butter or oil.
Lay a sheet of baking
paper over the greased
side of the foil. Pleat
them along the centre
2. Place the apple slices,
sugar and ¹/4 cup
(60 ml/2 fl oz) water in
a pan. Cover and cook
over a medium heat for
12 minutes, or until the
apple is soft but still
retains its shape. Cool.
Arrange the apple
slices, including any
liquid, in the base of
the prepared tin.
3. Place the chocolate in
a slow 150°C (300°F/
Gas 2) oven for
5 minutes, or until soft
but not hot. Remove
the chocolate from the
oven and increase the
temperature to 180°C
(350°F/Gas 4). Beat the
butter with electric
beaters for 1–2 minutes
until creamy, then beat
in the softened
chocolate, egg yolks
and caster sugar. Using
a large metal spoon, stir
in the milk then the
combined and sifted
flour, cocoa and
bicarbonate of soda
and the breadcrumbs.
4. In a clean bowl, beat
the egg whites until soft

peaks form. Stir a large
spoonful of egg white
through the chocolate
mixture to lighten it.
Fold the remaining egg
white through the
mixture until it is
smooth (do not
overmix). Spoon the
mixture into the tin and
smooth the surface.
5. Cover the top of the
tin with the greased foil
and paper, foil-side-up.
Secure with string.
Place the tin in a large
baking dish and pour in
enough hot water to
reach halfway up the
sides of the tin. Bake
for 55 minutes, or until
a skewer inserted into
the centre comes out
clean. Remove the tin
from the water and
remove the coverings.
Leave the pudding in
the tin for 5 minutes
before turning out onto
a serving plate. Serve
with hot Chocolate
Custard and
strawberries, if desired.
6. **To make Chocolate
Custard:** Place the
custard powder, sugar
and cocoa in a pan, add
a little milk and mix to
a smooth paste. Add
the remaining milk and
chocolate bits; stir over
medium heat for
3–4 minutes until it
thickens. Cover to
prevent a skin forming.

Chocolate Eve's Pudding with Chocolate Custard

Black Forest Pudding

Preparation time:
  35 minutes
Total cooking time:
  1 hour 55 minutes
Serves 6–8

425 g (13¹/2 oz) can
  pitted black cherries
1¹/2 cups (185 g/
  6 oz) self-raising
  flour
¹/2 cup (60 g/2 oz)
  plain flour
2 tablespoons cocoa
  powder
200 g (6¹/2 oz) butter
100 g (3¹/3 oz) dark
  chocolate, chopped
³/4 cup (140 g/4²/3 oz)
  lightly packed soft
  brown sugar
2 eggs, lightly beaten
1 tablespoon Kirsch
whipped cream,
  chocolate curls and
  maraschino cherries,
  to serve

1. Preheat the oven to
160°C (315°F/Gas
2–3). Lightly brush a
10 cup (2.5 litre)
capacity pudding basin
with melted butter or
oil; line the base with
baking paper. Drain the
cherries and reserve
¹/2 cup (125 ml/4 fl oz)
of the liquid. Spread
the cherries on a sheet
of paper towel and
pat dry.
2. Sift the flours and
cocoa powder into a
large bowl, add the
cherries and toss them
through. Make a well
in the centre. Place the
butter, chocolate, sugar
and reserved liquid
from the cherries in a
small pan. Stir over low
heat until the butter
and chocolate have
melted and the sugar
has dissolved.
3. Pour the melted
butter mixture into the

well in the dry
ingredients. Add the
eggs and stir gently
with a wooden spoon
until combined. Do not
overbeat, or the
pudding will be tough
and rubbery. Spoon the
mixture into the
prepared basin and
smooth the surface.
Bake for 1 hour
45 minutes, or until a
skewer comes out clean
when inserted into the
centre of the pudding.
4. Remove the pudding
from the oven and
pierce the top several
times with a skewer.
Pour the Kirsch over
the pudding and leave
for 5–10 minutes to
soak in. Turn the
pudding out of the
basin onto a serving
plate. Serve with
whipped cream,
chocolate curls and
maraschino cherries.

Black Forest Pudding

1 *Spread the cherries on a paper towel
and pat them dry.*

2 *Combine the butter, chocolate, sugar
and reserved liquid from the cherries.*

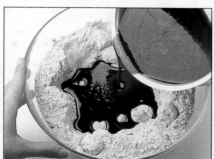

3 Pour the melted butter mixture into the well in the dry ingredients.

4 Pour the Kirsch over the top of the cooked pudding.

Harlequin Pudding with Cherry Kirsch Sauce

Preparation time:
45 minutes
Total cooking time:
1 hour 40 minutes
Serves 6–8

425 g (13¹/₂ oz) can
pitted black
cherries

Plain Batter
60 g (2 oz) butter
¹/₄ cup (60 g/2 oz)
caster sugar
1 egg
³/₄ cup (90 g/3 oz)
plain flour
¹/₄ cup (30 g/1 oz)
custard powder
1 teaspoon baking
powder
2 tablespoons milk
¹/₄ cup (45 g/1¹/₂ oz)
chocolate bits

Chocolate Batter
60 g (2 oz) butter
¹/₄ cup (60 g/2 oz)
caster sugar
1 egg
³/₄ cup (90 g/3 oz)
plain flour
¹/₄ cup (30 g/1 oz)
custard powder
1 teaspoon baking
powder
1 tablespoon cocoa
powder
3 tablespoons milk

Cherry Kirsch Sauce
3 teaspoons cornflour
reserved cherry juice
1–2 tablespoons Kirsch
thick cream, to serve

1. Brush a 7 cup
(1.75 litre) capacity
basin with melted
butter or oil. Brush a
large sheet of foil with
melted butter or oil.
Lay a sheet of baking
paper over the greased
side of the foil; pleat
along the centre. Drain
the cherries, reserving
the juice. Arrange the
cherries over the base
of the basin, adding a
tablespoon of juice.

**2. To make Plain
Batter:** Using electric
beaters, beat the butter
and sugar in a small
bowl for 2–3 minutes
until light and creamy.
Add the egg and beat
well. Fold in the sifted
flour, custard powder
and baking powder.
Fold in the milk. Spoon
the mixture over the
cherries in the basin.
Smooth the surface and
scatter over the
chocolate bits.

**3. To make Chocolate
Batter:** Beat the butter
and sugar with electric
beaters for 2–3 minutes
until light and creamy.
Add the egg and beat
well. Fold in the sifted
flour, custard powder,

baking powder and
cocoa. Fold in the milk.
4. Spoon the chocolate
mixture over the plain
batter. Cover with
greased foil and paper,
foil-side-up. Place the
lid over the foil and
secure the clips. If you
don't have a lid, lay a
pleated tea towel over
the foil; tie with string
under the lip. Knot the
corners together to act
as a handle.
5. Place the basin on a
trivet or an upturned
saucer in a large, deep
pan. Pour boiling water
down the side of the
pan to come halfway
up the side of the basin.
Bring to the boil, reduce
the heat slightly, cover
and simmer for 1 hour
30 minutes, or until a
skewer inserted into the
centre of the pudding
comes out clean. Add
more boiling water as
needed. Remove the
basin from the water.
Leave for 5 minutes
before turning out onto
a serving plate. Serve
hot with warm Cherry
Kirsch Sauce.
**6. To make Cherry
Kirsch Sauce:** In a pan,
mix the cornflour to a
smooth paste with a
tablespoon of water.
Add the reserved cherry
juice, stir over medium
heat for 3–4 minutes
until the sauce thickens.
Stir in Kirsch to taste.

Harlequin Pudding with Cherry Kirsch Sauce

Sticky Nutty Puddings with Hot Caramel Sauce

Preparation time:
45 minutes
Total cooking time:
1 hour
Serves 8

1 cup (180 g/5³/4 oz)
  dates, chopped
1 teaspoon vanilla
  essence
1/2 teaspoon
  bicarbonate of soda
1 cup (100 g/3¹/3 oz)
  pecans
90 g (3 oz) butter,
  softened
2/3 cup (160 g/5¹/4 oz)
  caster sugar
2 eggs, lightly beaten
1¹/2 cups (185 g/6 oz)
  self-raising flour
strawberries, to serve

Caramel Sauce
1 cup (185 g/6 oz)
  lightly packed soft
  brown sugar,
125 g (4 oz) butter,
  chopped
1/2 cup (125 ml/4 fl oz)
  cream

1. Preheat the oven to
180°C (350°F/Gas 4).
Lightly brush eight
1 cup (250 ml/8 fl oz)
capacity heatproof
moulds with melted

butter or oil; line the
bases with baking
paper. Brush 8 small
sheets of foil with
melted butter or oil.
Lay a small sheet of
baking paper over the
greased side of each
piece of foil and make a
pleat down the centre.
2. Place the dates in a
bowl and pour on
3/4 cup (185 ml/6 fl oz)
boiling water. Stir in the
vanilla essence and
bicarbonate of soda
and set aside (the
mixture will become
frothy). Lightly roast
the pecans under a
preheated medium grill.
Allow them to cool,
then chop roughly. Set
aside about a third
of the nuts to use as a
garnish. Beat the butter
and sugar with electric
beaters for 2–3 minutes
until light and creamy.
Add the eggs gradually,
beating well between
each addition. Using a
large metal spoon, fold
in the sifted flour, a
third at a time, then
stir through the
chopped nuts and the
date mixture.
3. Spoon the pudding
mixture evenly into the
prepared moulds and
smooth the surface.
Cover the top of each
mould with a piece
of greased foil and

paper, foil-side-up. Tie
with string. Place the
moulds in a large deep
baking dish. Carefully
pour boiling water
down the side of the
dish to come halfway
up the sides of the
moulds. Bake for
40 minutes, or until a
skewer inserted into
the centre of a pudding
comes out clean. Leave
the puddings to cool for
5 minutes in the
moulds. Gently loosen
the sides of each
pudding with a knife
before turning out onto
a baking dish. Reduce
the oven temperature to
160°C (315°F/
Gas 2–3).
**4. To make Caramel
Sauce:** Place the sugar,
butter and cream in a
small pan and stir over
low heat for 5 minutes,
or until the sugar has
completely dissolved.
Spoon 2 tablespoons
of the sauce over each
pudding. Return
the puddings to the
oven for 10 minutes to
heat them through and
allow them to absorb
some of the sauce. Serve
the puddings on large
individual plates with
the extra warmed
Caramel Sauce,
strawberries and a
sprinkling of the
reserved nuts.

Sticky Nutty Puddings with Hot Caramel Sauce

Mango Upside-down Steamed Pudding

Preparation time:
  35 minutes
Total cooking time:
  1 hour 30 minutes
Serves 4–6

3 tablespoons sugar
1 x 425 g (13^1/2 oz) can
  mangoes in natural
  juices
100 g (3^1/3 oz) soft
  butter
^{1}/2 cup (125 g/4 oz)
  caster sugar
^{1}/2 teaspoon grated
  lime rind
2 eggs
1 cup (125 g/4 oz) self-
  raising flour
3 tablespoons ground
  almonds
pinch of crushed
  cardamom seeds
1 tablespoon lime juice
2 teaspoons arrowroot

1. Brush a 6 cup
(1.5 litre) capacity glass
or ceramic pudding
basin with melted
butter or oil. Don't use
a metal dish or the
pudding will stick. Line
the base with baking
paper; grease the paper.
Brush a large sheet of
foil with melted butter
or oil. Lay a sheet of

baking paper over the
greased side of the foil.
Pleat them along the
centre.
2. Combine the sugar
and 3 tablespoons of
water in a pan; stir over
low heat until the sugar
has dissolved. Bring to
the boil, reduce the
heat and simmer,
without stirring, until
the mixture turns a
golden caramel colour.
(This should take about
6 minutes: watch
carefully as it can burn
quickly.) As soon as
the mixture has turned
golden, pour it quickly
into the pudding basin.
Set aside.
3. Drain and reserve
the juice from the
mangoes. Cut 5 long
strips of mango and set
aside; roughly chop the
rest. Beat the butter,
sugar and lime rind in a
small bowl until light
and creamy. Add the
eggs one at a time
beating well after each
addition. Transfer to a
large bowl. Fold in half
the flour and the
chopped mango. Add
the remaining flour,
ground almonds and
cardamom; mix well.
4. Take the reserved
strips of mango and
arrange in a single layer
on the caramel in the
base of the pudding

basin. Spoon the
pudding mixture into
the basin. Cover with
the greased foil and
paper, foil-side-up.
Place the lid over the
foil and secure the
clips. If you have no
lid, lay a pleated tea
towel over the foil and
tie with string under
the lip of the basin.
Knot the corners
together to act as a
handle to lower the
basin into the pan.
5. Place the basin on a
trivet or an upturned
saucer in a large deep
pan. Pour boiling water
down the side of the
pan to come halfway
up the basin. Bring to
the boil, reduce the
heat slightly, cover and
simmer for 1 hour
15 minutes. When
cooked, the pudding
should appear well
risen and feel firm to
the touch.
6. While the pudding is
cooking, make the
sauce: place the
reserved mango juices
in a pan; add the lime
juice. Whisk in the
arrowroot and cook
over gentle heat,
stirring constantly, until
the sauce boils,
thickens and becomes
clear. Loosen the
pudding from the basin
with a knife before
turning out. Serve with
the warm mango sauce.

Mango Upside-down Steamed Pudding

Sticky Apple Gingerbread Pudding with Brandy Cream Sauce

Preparation time:
  25 minutes
Total cooking time:
  1 hour 25 minutes
Serves 8–10

125 g (4 oz) butter
1/2 cup (125 g/4 oz)
  caster sugar
1 cup (350 g/11 1/4 oz)
  golden syrup
2 eggs
2 cups (250 g/8 oz)
  plain flour
3 teaspoons ground
  ginger
1 teaspoon mixed
  spice
1/4 teaspoon ground
  cloves
1 teaspoon bicarbonate
  of soda
2 green apples,
  peeled, cored and
  chopped

Brandy Cream Sauce
1 1/2 cups (375 ml/
  12 fl oz) cream
1/4 cup (90 g/3 oz)
  golden syrup
1 1/2 tablespoons
  brandy

1. Preheat the oven to 160°C (315°F/Gas 2–3). Lightly brush a 23 cm (9 inch) square cake tin with melted butter or oil; line the base with baking paper.
2. Combine the butter, sugar and golden syrup in a large pan and stir over medium heat until the butter has melted, the sugar has dissolved and the mixture is smooth. Remove from the heat, cool slightly and, using a wire whisk, beat in the eggs.
3. Sift the flour, ginger, mixed spice, ground cloves and bicarbonate of soda together and, using the wire whisk, stir into the butter mixture alternately with 1 cup (250 ml/ 8 fl oz) hot water; turning gently until the mixture is just combined. Don't overbeat at this stage or the pudding will be tough and rubbery.
4. Pour the mixture into the prepared tin, and sprinkle the chopped apple over the top. Bake for 1 hour 15 minutes, or until a skewer inserted into the centre of the pudding comes out clean. Leave for 3 minutes before turning out onto a wire rack to cool. Make the sauce while the pudding is cooking.

4. To make Brandy Cream Sauce: Combine the cream and golden syrup in a small pan, stir over medium heat and bring to the boil. Reduce the heat and simmer uncovered for 1 minute. Remove from the heat and stir in the brandy. Serve the pudding warm or at room temperature, with the warm Brandy Cream Sauce.

Note: This pudding tastes even better when made a day in advance, as this allows the flavours to develop. Cool the pudding completely and store in an airtight container overnight. To serve warm, place on an ovenproof plate, cover with foil and reheat gently in a warm 160°C (315°F/Gas 2–3) oven. The Brandy Cream Sauce is best made close to serving time.

Sticky Apple Gingerbread Pudding with Brandy Cream Sauce

Sticky Marshmallow and Chocolate Whisky Pudding

Preparation time:
  30 minutes
Total cooking time:
  1 hour
Serves 6–8

2 cups (250 g/8 oz) self-
  raising flour
1/2 cup (60 g/2 oz) plain
  flour
1/3 cup (40 g/1¹/3 oz)
  dark cocoa
150 g (4³/4 oz) butter,
  chopped
200 g (6¹/2 oz) dark
  chocolate, chopped
1/3 cup (80 ml/
  2³/4 fl oz) whisky
1/2 cup (125 g/4 oz)
  caster sugar
3/4 cup (185 g/6 oz)
  sour cream
2 eggs, lightly beaten
150 g (4³/4 oz) white
  marshmallows, cut
  into quarters
icing sugar, thick cream
  and strawberries, to
  serve

1. Preheat the oven to
160°C (315°F/
Gas 2–3). Lightly brush
a 20 cm (8 inch) square
tin with melted butter
or oil; line the base
with baking paper.
Brush a large sheet of
foil with melted butter

or oil. Lay a sheet of
baking paper over the
greased side of the foil.
Pleat them along the
centre.
2. Sift the flours and
cocoa together in a
large mixing bowl and
make a well in the
centre. Place the butter,
chocolate, whisky, sugar
and cream in a pan. Stir
over low heat until the
butter and chocolate
have melted and all the
ingredients are blended.
Cool slightly.
3. Whisk the eggs into
the mixture in the pan.
Pour the chocolate
mixture into the flours.
Whisk until all the
ingredients are
combined; do not
overbeat. Fold through
the marshmallows. The
mixture will appear
quite thick.
4. Spoon the mixture
into the prepared tin,
ensuring that the
marshmallows near the
edge are well coated.
Smooth the surface and
cover the tin with the
greased foil and paper,
foil-side-up. Bake for
1 hour, or until a
skewer inserted into
the centre of the
pudding comes out
clean. Turn the pudding
out onto a serving plate.
Dust with icing sugar.
Serve in slices with
thick cream and fresh
strawberries.

Honeycomb Pudding

Preparation time:
  25 minutes
Total cooking time:
  50 minutes
Serves 6–8

125 g (4 oz) butter
1/4 cup (60 g/2 oz)
  caster sugar
2 eggs, lightly
  beaten
1 teaspoon vanilla
  essence
1³/4 cups (220 g/7 oz)
  self-raising flour
3/4 cup (185 ml/6 fl oz)
  milk
150 g (4³/4 oz) fresh
  honeycomb, roughly
  chopped
thick cream and
  fresh honeycomb,
  to serve

1. Preheat the oven to
180°C (350°F/Gas 4).
Brush a deep 6 cup
(1.5 litre) capacity
round ovenproof bowl
with melted butter or
oil; line the base with
baking paper.
2. Using electric
beaters, beat the butter
and sugar until light
and creamy. Gradually
add the eggs and vanilla
essence, beating well
after each addition.
3. Using a large metal
spoon, fold in the sifted
flour alternately with

Honeycomb Pudding (top) with Sticky Marshmallow and Chocolate Whisky Pudding

the milk until just combined. Fold in the chopped honeycomb. Spoon the mixture into the prepared pudding bowl. Bake for 45–50 minutes, or until a skewer inserted into the centre of the pudding comes out clean. Turn the pudding out of the bowl onto a servng plate and serve with thick cream and the extra honeycomb. Drizzle the top of the pudding with honey from the honeycomb.

Ginger Pudding with Sherry Mousseline

Preparation time:
35 minutes
Total cooking time:
2 hours 40 minutes
Serves 6–8

100 g (3^1/3 oz)
crystallised ginger,
roughly chopped
2^1/2 cups (310 g/
9^3/4 oz) plain flour
1 teaspoon bicarbonate
of soda
1 teaspoon ground
ginger
^{1}/4 teaspoon mixed
spice
125 g (4 oz) butter,
chopped
1 egg, lightly beaten
^{3}/4 cup (185 ml/6 fl oz)
milk, warmed
^{3}/4 cup (260 g/8^1/2 oz)
golden syrup,
warmed
1 tablespoon golden
syrup, extra

Sherry Mousseline
1 egg
1 egg yolk
2 tablespoons caster
sugar
2 tablespoons sherry

1. Lightly brush an
8 cup (2 litre) capacity
heatproof pudding
basin with melted
butter or oil. Brush a
large sheet of foil with
melted butter or oil.
Lay a sheet of baking
paper over the greased
side of the foil. Pleat
them along the centre.
Sprinkle the chopped
crystallised ginger
over the bottom of
the basin.
2. Sift the flour,
bicarbonate of soda,
ground ginger and
mixed spice into a large
bowl. Add the chopped
butter and, with your
fingertips, rub in the
butter until it is fine
and crumbly. Make a
well in the centre of the
mixture and add the
beaten egg, milk and
golden syrup all at
once. Stir until the
mixture is well
combined; be careful
not to overbeat.
3. Pour the mixture
into the prepared basin.
Cover with the greased
foil and paper, foil-side-
up. Place the lid over
the foil and secure the
clips. If you don't have
a lid, lay a pleated tea
towel over the foil, tie
securely with string
under the lip of the
basin and knot the four
corners together; this
acts as a handle to help
lower the basin into
the pan.
4. Place the basin on a
trivet or an upturned
saucer in a large,
deep pan. Carefully
pour boiling water
down the side of the
pan to come halfway
up the side of the basin.
Bring to the boil then
reduce the heat slightly.
Cover the pan and
simmer for 2 hours
30 minutes, or until a
skewer inserted into
the centre of the
pudding comes out
clean. Add more
boiling water to the
pan as necessary: do
not let it boil dry.
Remove the pudding
basin from the water
and remove the
coverings. Leave the
pudding in the basin
for 5 minutes before
turning it out onto a
large serving plate.
Spoon the extra golden
syrup over the top of
the pudding to give the
ginger a gloss. Serve
hot with Sherry
Mousseline and thick
cream, if liked.
**5. To make Sherry
Mousseline:** Combine
the egg, egg yolk, sugar
and sherry in a
heatproof bowl and
stand it over a pan of
just simmering water.
Using electric beaters,
beat continuously for
5–8 minutes, or until
the mixture becomes
thick and frothy. Serve
immediately.

Ginger Pudding with Sherry Mousseline

Custards and Sauces

I f your pudding recipe doesn't have its own sauce, choose between a creamy custard, a richly flavoured sauce or a refreshing fruit coulis for the perfect finishing touch.

Easy Vanilla Custard

Combine 1 cup (250 ml/ 8 fl oz) milk and 1/4 cup (60 ml/2 fl oz) cream in a medium pan. Bring to boiling point, then remove from the heat immediately. In a bowl, whisk 3 egg yolks, 1/2 cup (125 g/4 oz) caster sugar and 2 teaspoons cornflour. Slowly pour the hot milk and cream onto the egg mixture, whisking continuously. Return to the pan and stir over a low heat for 5 minutes or until thickened—do not boil. Remove from the heat and stir in 1/2 teaspoon vanilla essence. Makes 2 1/4 cups (560ml/ 18 fl oz).

Hot Chocolate Sauce

In a small pan, combine 1 cup (250 ml/8 fl oz) cream, 30 g (1 oz) butter and 200 g (6 1/2 oz) chopped dark chocolate. Stir over low heat until the butter and chocolate are completely melted and the mixture is smooth. Serve the sauce hot or at room temperature. Makes 2 cups (500 ml/ 16 fl oz).

Easy Fruit Coulis

Place 500 g (1 lb) strawberries in a food processor. Add about a tablespoon of icing sugar, according to taste, and process until liquid. Strain the mixture through a sieve to remove the seeds if desired. As a variation, blueberries, raspberries or the equivalent weight in soft fruits such as mangoes or kiwi fruit, can be used. Frozen berries are also suitable. Also serve over ice cream, mousses, or with meringues and sliced fruit. Makes about 1 1/4 cups (315 ml/10 fl oz).

Crème Anglaise

Split a vanilla bean lengthways and place in a small pan with 1 1/2 cups (375 ml/ 12 fl oz) milk. Heat until almost boiling and set aside for 10 minutes to infuse. Whisk 3 egg yolks and 2 tablespoons sugar for about 3 minutes, until light and creamy. Remove the vanilla bean and pour the milk onto the egg mixture, stirring constantly. Return to the pan, stir over low heat for about 5 minutes, until thickened—do not boil or it will curdle. The custard should coat the back of a spoon when ready. Makes about 1 3/4 cups (440 ml/14 fl oz).

Custards and Sauces, from left: Easy Vanilla Custard; Easy Fruit Coulis; Hot Chocolate Sauce; Crème Anglaise.

Custard Pudding with Stewed Apples

Preparation time:
  25 minutes
Total cooking time:
  2 1/2 hours
Serves 6

Custard
1 1/2 tablespoons
  custard powder
1/2 cup (125 ml/4 fl oz)
  milk
1 tablespoon sugar
1/3 cup (90 g/3 oz) sour
  cream

180 g (5 3/4 oz) butter
1/2 cup (125 g/4 oz)
  caster sugar
2 eggs
1 1/4 cups (155 g/5 oz)
  self-raising flour
1/4 cup (30 g/1 oz)
  custard powder
1/4 cup (45 g/1 1/2 oz)
  ground almonds
1 cup (250 ml/8 fl oz)
  cream
4 green apples
2 tablespoons sugar
icing sugar, for dusting

1. To make the Custard:
Combine the custard
powder and a little
of the milk in a bowl
and mix until smooth.
Add the remaining milk
and mix together. Pour
into a pan, add the
sugar and cream. Stir
over medium heat until
the custard thickens
and boils. Remove from
the heat; cover the
surface with plastic
wrap to prevent a skin
forming.
2. Preheat the oven to
180°C (350°F/Gas 4).
Beat the butter and
sugar together until
light and creamy. Add
the eggs one at a time,
beating well after each
addition. Fold in the
sifted flour, custard
powder and ground
almonds alternately
with the cream.
3. Place half the
pudding mixture in an
8 cup (2 litre) capacity
ovenproof dish; spoon
the custard over it. Top
with the remaining
pudding mixture. The
mixture will be a little
stiff, pile it on top of
the custard and smooth
it out gently with the
back of a spoon. Bake
for 45–50 minutes, or
until the pudding is
firm to the touch.
4. Meanwhile, peel,
core and thinly slice the
apples and place in a
pan with the sugar and
2 tablespoons of water.
Bring to the boil,
reduce the heat and
simmer, covered, for
10 minutes, until the
apples are tender. Serve
the pudding from the
dish, accompanied by
the warm apples.

Ricotta Pudding with Strawberry Maple Syrup Sauce

Preparation time:
  30 minutes
Total cooking time:
  1 hour
Serves 6–8

500 g (1 lb) fresh ricotta
3/4 cup (185 g/6 oz)
  caster sugar
3 eggs
3 teaspoons grated
  lemon rind
1 1/2 cups (185 g/6 oz)
  self-raising flour, sifted
1/4 cup (60 ml/2 fl oz)
  lemon juice

*Strawberry Maple
Syrup Sauce*
1 cup (250 ml/8 fl oz)
  maple syrup
1 cup (150 g/4 3/4 oz)
  sliced strawberries

1. Preheat the oven to
180°C (350°F/Gas 4).
Brush a 20 cm (8 inch)
square tin with melted
butter or oil; line the
base with baking paper.
2. Beat the ricotta and
sugar with electric
beaters until smooth.
Add the eggs gradually,
beating well after each
addition. Add the lemon
rind and mix well. Fold
in the flour and lemon
juice. Spoon the
mixture into the tin;

Custard Pudding with Stewed Apples (top) and Ricotta Pudding with Strawberry Maple Syrup Sauce

bake for 55 minutes. When a skewer is inserted into the centre of the pudding, it should come out with a moist crumb. If the skewer is clean the pudding will be too dry. Leave in the tin for 10 minutes before turning out. Dust with icing sugar, cut into squares and place on serving plates.

3. To make Strawberry

Maple Syrup Sauce: Place the maple syrup in a pan over low heat, add the strawberries, and warm. Spoon the syrup and strawberries over the pudding.

49

Sweet Potato Pudding with Orange Cream

Preparation time:
35 minutes
Total cooking time:
1 hour 35 minutes
Serves 6

2 cups (250 g/8 oz)
   self-raising flour
1 teaspoon ground
   nutmeg
125g (4 oz) butter
³/4 cup (165 g/5¹/2 oz)
   firmly packed soft
   brown sugar
2 eggs, lightly
   beaten
¹/4 cup (60 ml/2 fl oz)
   cream
1 cup (250 g/8 oz)
   cooked and mashed
   orange sweet
   potato (see Note)

Orange Cream
300 g (9²/3 oz) sour
   cream
2 tablespoons soft
   brown sugar
1 tablespoon Grand
   Marnier

1. Lightly brush an 8 cup (2 litre) capacity pudding basin with melted butter or oil; line the base with baking paper. Brush a large sheet of foil with melted butter or oil. Lay a sheet of baking paper over the greased side of the foil. Pleat them along the centre.

2. Sift the flour and ground nutmeg into a large mixing bowl. Place the butter and sugar in a small pan and stir over a low heat until the butter has melted and the sugar has dissolved. Remove from the heat and allow the mixture to cool slightly. Add the melted butter mixture, the eggs and cream to the dry ingredients and, using a wooden spoon, stir until the mixture is thoroughly combined. Stir in the cooled sweet potato; be careful not to overbeat or the pudding will be tough.

3. Spoon the mixture into the prepared basin and smooth the surface. Cover with the greased foil and paper, foil-side-up. Place the lid over the foil and secure the clips. If you don't have a lid, lay a pleated tea towel over the foil; tie it securely with string under the lip of the basin and knot the four corners together; this will act as a handle to help you lower the basin into the pan.

4. Place the basin on a trivet or an upturned saucer in a large, deep pan. Carefully pour boiling water down the side of the pan to come halfway up the side of the basin. Bring to the boil, reduce the heat slightly and simmer, covered, for 1¹/2 hours, or until a skewer inserted into the centre of the pudding comes out clean. Add more boiling water to the pan as necessary: do not let it boil dry.

5. **To make Orange Cream:** Place the sour cream, sugar and Grand Marnier in a bowl and mix until well combined. Serve the Sweet Potato Pudding immediately with a spoonful of the Orange Cream.

Note: You will need to boil or steam 375 g (12 oz) of raw sweet potato for this recipe. Make sure the potato is well drained before it is mashed.

HINT
Pumpkin could replace the sweet potato in this recipe. Butternut pumpkin will give a lovely flavour, though any variety would suit.

Sweet Potato Pudding with Orange Cream

1 Using a flat-bladed knife, mix in almost all of the cream.

2 Drizzle 2 tablespoons of passionfruit pulp over the dough.

Sticky Orange and Passionfruit Swirled Pudding

Preparation time:
35 minutes +
20 minutes chilling
Total cooking time:
55 minutes
Serves 6

3 cups (375 g/12 oz)
plain flour
1¹/2 teaspoons baking
powder
pinch of salt
200 g (6¹/2 oz)
chilled butter,
chopped
¹/2 cup (45 g/1¹/2 oz)
desiccated coconut
300 ml (9¹/2 fl oz)
cream
¹/2 cup (160 g/
5¹/4 oz) orange
marmalade
2 tablespoons
passionfruit pulp

Passionfruit Syrup
¹/2 cup (125 ml/4 fl oz)
orange juice
³/4 cup (185 g/6 oz)
caster sugar
¹/4 cup (60 g/2 oz)
passionfruit pulp

1. Sift the flour, baking powder and salt into a mixing bowl. Rub in the butter with your fingertips until fine and crumbly. Stir in the coconut. With a flat-bladed knife, mix in most of the cream. Add the rest, if needed, when the mixture is almost together. Press together to form a soft dough; roll between 2 sheets of baking paper to make a 25 x 40 cm (10 x 16 inch) rectangle.
2. Spread marmalade over the dough; drizzle over the passionfruit pulp. Roll up lengthways like a swiss roll. Refrigerate for 20 minutes until firm.
3. Preheat the oven to 180°C (350°F/Gas 4). Brush a deep 20 cm (8 inch) round cake tin with melted butter or oil; line the base with baking paper. Cut the rolled dough into 2 cm (³/4 inch) slices; arrange half over the base of the tin. Place a second layer over the gaps where the bottom slices join. Place the tin on a baking tray.
4. **To make Passionfruit Syrup:** Place the orange juice, sugar, passionfruit pulp and ¹/4 cup (60 ml/2 fl oz) water in a pan. Stir over low heat, without boiling, until the sugar has dissolved. Bring to the boil; pour the syrup over the pudding. Bake for 50 minutes, until a skewer comes out clean. Leave for 15 minutes before turning out onto a serving dish.

Sticky Orange and Passionfruit Swirled Pudding

3 Cut the rolled up dough into 2 cm (³/4 inch) slices.

4 Pour the Passionfruit Syrup over the pudding.

53

Pear and Apple Pudding

Preparation time:
  40 minutes
Total cooking time:
  1 hour 50 minutes
Serves 6–8

1 pear, firm but ripe
1 green apple
120 g (4 oz) butter
1/4 cup (45 g/1 1/2 oz)
  lightly packed soft
  brown sugar
1/2 cup (125 g/4 oz)
  caster sugar
2 eggs, lightly beaten
1 teaspoon vanilla
  essence
1 1/2 cups (185 g/6 oz)
  self-raising flour
1/3 cup (80 ml/
  2 3/4 fl oz) buttermilk

Vanilla Custard
1 1/2 cups (375 ml/
  12 fl oz) milk
3 egg yolks
1/4 cup (60 g/2 oz)
  caster sugar
2 teaspoons cornflour
1/2 teaspoon vanilla
  essence

1. Brush a 10 cup
(2.5 litre) capacity
pudding basin with
melted butter or oil;
line the base with
baking paper. Brush a
large sheet of foil with
melted butter or oil.
Lay a sheet of baking
paper over the greased
side of the foil. Pleat
them along the centre.
2. Peel, core and slice
the pear and apple.
Place 30 g (1 oz) of the
butter and the brown
sugar in a frying pan;
stir over medium heat
until the sugar has
dissolved. Add the
sliced pear and apple to
the pan and increase
the heat to medium
high. Cook for about
5 minutes, stirring
occasionally until the
fruit is golden brown.
Spoon the fruit, and
butter mixture into the
prepared basin.
3. Using electric
beaters, beat the
remaining butter and
the caster sugar until
light and creamy.
Gradually add the eggs,
beating well after each
addition. Beat in the
vanilla essence. Fold in
the sifted flour
alternately with the
buttermilk until just
combined.
4. Spoon the mixture
into the basin. Cover
with the greased foil
and paper, foil-side-up.
Place the lid over the
foil and secure the
clips. If you don't have
a lid, lay a pleated tea
towel over the foil, tie
securely with string
under the lip of the
basin and knot the four
corners together; this
acts as a handle to help
lower the basin into the
pan. Place the basin on
a trivet or an upturned
saucer in a large,
deep pan.
5. Pour boiling water
down the side of the
pan to come halfway
up the side of the basin.
Bring to the boil,
reduce the heat slightly,
cover and simmer for
1 1/2 hours, or until a
skewer inserted into the
centre of the pudding
comes out clean. Add
more boiling water to
the pan as necessary:
do not let it boil dry.
Turn out and serve with
Vanilla Custard.
**6. To make Vanilla
Custard:** Place the milk
in a pan, bring just to
the boil then remove
from the heat. Beat the
egg yolks, sugar and
cornflour together in a
bowl with a wire whisk
until thick and creamy.
Gradually beat in the
milk. Return the
mixture to a clean pan
and stir over low heat
for 15 minutes, or until
the custard thickens
and coats the back of a
spoon. Stir in the
vanilla. Strain into a
jug; cover with a disc of
baking paper to prevent
a skin from forming.

Pear and Apple Pudding

Pineapple Butterscotch Pudding with Yoghurt Cream

Preparation time:
40 minutes
Total cooking time:
50 minutes
Serves 6–8

Butterscotch Mixture
60 g (2 oz) butter
$1/2$ cup (95 g/$3^1/4$ oz)
    lightly packed soft
    brown sugar
440 g (14 oz) canned
    pineapple rings,
    drained

Pudding Mixture
185 g (6 oz) butter
$1/2$ cup (125 g/4 oz)
    caster sugar
1 teaspoon vanilla
    essence
3 eggs
2 cups (250 g/8 oz)
    self-raising flour

Yoghurt Cream
1 cup (250 ml/8 fl oz)
    cream
1 tablespoon soft
    brown sugar
200 ml ($6^1/2$ fl oz) plain
    yoghurt

1. Preheat the oven to
180°C (350°F/Gas 4).

Lightly brush an 8 cup (2 litre) fluted ring tin with melted butter or oil. Brush a large sheet of foil with melted butter or oil. Lay a sheet of baking paper over the greased side of the foil. Pleat them along the centre.
2. To make the Butterscotch Mixture: Beat the butter with electric beaters for 5–7 minutes until pale. Add the brown sugar; beat for a further 2 minutes until thick and creamy. Using a spatula, carefully spread the mixture over the base and about 2 cm ($3/4$ inch) up the side of the tin. Arrange the drained pineapple rings at intervals around the base. You will need 5 rings.
3. To make Pudding Mixture: Beat the butter, caster sugar and vanilla essence with electric beaters for 5–6 minutes until light and creamy. Add the eggs one at a time, beating well between each addition. Fold in the sifted flour, a third at a time, using a large metal spoon.
4. Spoon the mixture into the prepared tin and smooth the surface,

taking care not to dislodge the pineapple rings. Cover with the greased foil and paper, foil-side-up, and secure with string. Place the tin in a large baking pan and pour in hot water to come halfway up the side of the tin. Bake for 50 minutes, or until a skewer inserted into the centre of the pudding comes out clean. Leave in the tin for 5 minutes before turning out onto a serving plate. Serve the pudding hot with Yoghurt Cream and strawberries, if desired.
5. To make Yoghurt Cream: Beat the cream and brown sugar until soft peaks form; fold in the yoghurt. Cover and refrigerate until required. Yoghurt Cream can be made several hours before serving. It will thicken on standing.

> HINT
> To soften brown sugar place it in a microwave-proof dish, add a slice of soft white bread or a wedge of apple, cover tightly and microwave on High (100%) for 30 seconds. Discard the bread or apple and stir.

Pineapple Butterscotch Pudding with Yoghurt Cream

Sticky Chocolate and Nut Puddings with Chocolate Liqueur Sauce

Preparation time:
  45 minutes
Total cooking time:
  55 minutes
Makes 6

100 g (3¹/3 oz) dark
  chocolate, chopped
100 g (3¹/3 oz) butter,
  softened
4 eggs, separated
¹/3 cup (90 g/3 oz)
  caster sugar
¹/3 cup (35 g/1¹/4 oz)
  ground hazelnuts
¹/2 cup (40 g/1¹/3 oz)
  cake or bread crumbs
¹/2 cup (60 g/2 oz) plain
  flour
60 g (2 oz) roasted
  hazelnuts, skinned
  and chopped
thick cream, to serve

Chocolate Liqueur Sauce
200 g (6¹/2 oz) dark
  chocolate, chopped
1 cup (250 ml/8 fl oz)
  cream
1–2 tablespoons liqueur
  (see Note)

1. Lightly brush six
1 cup (250 ml/8 fl oz)
capacity heatproof
moulds (metal dariole
moulds or ceramic
ramekins) with melted
butter or oil; line the
bases with baking
paper. Brush 6 small
sheets of foil with
melted butter or oil.
Lay a small sheet of
baking paper over the
greased side of each
piece of foil and make a
pleat down the centre.
2. Place the chocolate
in a heatproof bowl
and place in a slow
150°C (300°F/Gas 4)
oven for 5 minutes, or
until the chocolate is
soft but not hot or
melted. Remove the
chocolate and increase
the oven temperature
to 180°C (350°F/
Gas 4).
3. Beat the butter with
electric beaters for
1–2 minutes or until it
is light and creamy.
Then beat in the
softened chocolate, the
egg yolks and half the
sugar. Using a large
metal spoon, stir in the
ground hazelnuts, cake
or bread crumbs and
the sifted flour.
4. In a clean, dry bowl,
beat the egg whites with
electric beaters until
firm peaks form. Add
the remaining sugar
and beat for a further
minute. Stir a large
spoonful of the beaten
egg white into the
chocolate mixture, this
will make it softer and
lighter, then carefully
fold the remaining egg
white into the mixture
until it is just combined.
Be careful not to
overmix, or you will
lose the volume from
the beaten egg whites.
5. Spoon the mixture
evenly into the
prepared moulds and
carefully smooth the
surface. Cover each
mould with a piece of
greased foil and paper,
foil-side-up. Secure
with string. Place the
moulds in a large
baking dish and
carefully pour boiling
water down the side of
the dish to come
halfway up the sides of
the moulds. Bake for
40 minutes, or until a
skewer inserted into the
centre of a pudding
comes out clean. Leave
the puddings in their
moulds for 5 minutes,
before turning them out
onto individual serving
plates. Serve warm
with the Chocolate
Liqueur Sauce, a
sprinkling of chopped
roasted hazelnuts and
thick cream.
6. To make Chocolate
Liqueur Sauce: Place
the chocolate and
cream in a small pan.
Stir over a low heat,
until the chocolate has
completely melted
and the mixture is
smooth, then stir in the
liqueur, to taste.

Sticky Chocolate and Nut Puddings with Chocolate Liqueur Sauce

Note: Any liqueur or brandy can be used in the Chocolate Liqueur Sauce, use whichever you prefer. Tia Maria, Kahlua or Frangelico would all suit the recipe very well. To roast the hazelnuts: place them under a preheated moderately hot grill for about 3–4 minutes until they are lightly browned; be careful not to burn them. Place the roasted hazelnuts in a clean tea towel and rub off the skins.

Pear and Almond Steamed Pudding

Preparation time:
  20 minutes
Total cooking time:
  1 hour 50 minutes
Serves 6

100 g (3¹/2 oz) soft
  butter
²/3 cup (160 g/5¹/4 oz)
  caster sugar
3 eggs
2 ripe pears
3 tablespoons
  ground almonds
1¹/4 cups (155 g/5 oz)
  self-raising flour
1 tablespoon
  Amaretto
1 tablespoon flaked
  almonds
toasted flaked almonds,
  and strawberries, to
  serve

Almond Custard
4 egg yolks
¹/4 cup (60 g/2 oz)
  caster sugar
1 teaspoon cornflour
1¹/2 cups (375 ml/
  12 fl oz) milk
¹/2 cup (125 ml/4 fl oz)
  cream
almond essence, to
  taste

1. Lightly brush a 6 cup
(1 litre) capacity
pudding basin with
melted butter or oil;
line the base with
baking paper. Brush a
large sheet of foil with
melted butter or oil.
Lay a sheet of baking
paper over the greased
side of the foil. Pleat
them along the centre.
2. Using electric
beaters, beat the butter
and sugar until pale.
Add the eggs one at a
time to the mixture,
beating well after each
addition. Peel, core and
roughly chop the pears,
stir in, along with the
ground almonds.
Gently fold in the flour,
Amaretto and flaked
almonds; stir until
combined.
3. Spoon the mixture
into the prepared basin
and cover with the
greased foil and paper.
Place the pudding basin
lid over the foil and
secure the clips. If you
don't have a lid, lay a
pleated tea towel over
the foil, tie securely
with string under the
lip of the basin and
knot the four corners
together; this will act as
a handle to help lower
the basin into the pan.
4. Place the basin on a
trivet or an upturned
saucer in a large deep
pan. Carefully pour
boiling water down the
side of the pan to come
halfway up the side of
the basin. Bring to the
boil, reduce the heat
slightly, cover and
simmer for 1 hour
40 minutes, or until a
skewer inserted into the
centre of the pudding
comes out clean. Add
more boiling water to
the pan as necessary
during cooking: do not
let the pan boil dry.
5. Carefully loosen the
side of the pudding
with a flat-bladed knife
before turning it out of
the basin and onto a
large serving plate.
Serve with Almond
Custard, flaked almonds
and strawberries.
**6. To make Almond
Custard:** Whisk the egg
yolks, sugar and
cornflour together for
2 minutes or until
creamy. Place the milk
and cream in a pan and
heat slowly until the
mixture just reaches
boiling point. Pour the
hot milk and cream
mixture slowly over the
beaten egg yolks and
sugar, whisking
constantly. Return the
mixture to a clean pan
and stir gently over low
heat until it has
thickened and will coat
the back of a metal
spoon. Add a few drops
of almond essence, to
taste. Do not boil the
Almond Custard or it
will curdle.

Pear and Almond Steamed Pudding

Chocolate Hazelnut Pudding with Marsala Mascarpone Cream

Preparation time:
  15 minutes
Total cooking time:
  1 hour 45 minutes
Serves 6

100 g (3¹/3 oz) butter
¹/3 cup (90 g/3 oz)
  caster sugar
2 tablespoons
  Marsala
4 eggs, separated
125 g (4 oz) dark
  chocolate, melted
  and cooled slightly
¹/2 cup (60 g/2 oz)
  plain flour
³/4 cup (80 g/
  2²/3 oz) ground
  hazelnuts
¹/2 cup (40 g/1¹/3 oz)
  stale breadcrumbs
¹/4 cup (60 g/2 oz)
  caster sugar, extra

**Marsala Mascarpone
  Cream**
250 g (8 oz)
  mascarpone
2 tablespoons
  Marsala
150 g (4³/4 oz) dark
  chocolate, melted
  and cooled slightly

1. Lightly brush a 6 cup (1.5 litre) capacity pudding basin with melted butter or oil; line the base with baking paper. Brush a large sheet of foil with melted butter or oil. Lay a sheet of baking paper over the greased side of the foil. Pleat them along the centre.
2. Beat the butter, sugar and Marsala in a bowl with electric beaters until light and creamy. Add the egg yolks one at a time, beating well between each addition. Beat in the chocolate. Using a metal spoon fold in the flour, nuts and breadcrumbs.
3. Beat the egg whites in a clean bowl with electric beaters until soft peaks form. Gradually beat in the extra sugar, adding 1 tablespoon at a time. Beat until the mixture is thick, glossy and the sugar has dissolved. Using a large metal spoon, carefully fold the egg white mixture into the chocolate mixture in two batches, until just combined.
4. Spoon the mixture into the pudding basin and cover with the greased foil and paper, foil-side-up. Place the

lid over the foil and secure the clips. If you have no lid, lay a pleated tea towel over the foil, tie with string under the lip of the basin and knot the four corners together; this acts as a handle to help lower the basin into the pan.
5. Place the basin on a trivet or an upturned saucer in a large, deep pan. Pour boiling water down the side of the pan to come halfway up the side of the basin. Bring to the boil, reduce the heat slightly and simmer, covered, for 1 hour 45 minutes, or until a skewer inserted into the centre of the pudding comes out clean. Leave the pudding for 5 minutes before turning out onto a serving plate. Serve warm with Marsala Mascarpone cream.
6. To make Marsala Mascarpone Cream: Soften the mascarpone with a spoon or whisk and gradually mix in the Marsala and melted chocolate.

Note: Try to have the mascarpone at room temperature when mixing in the chocolate: this will help prevent the chocolate from setting too quickly.

Chocolate Hazelnut Pudding with Marsala Mascarpone Cream

Index